Souvenir and

The Hope Valley

Louise Maskill

CURLEW
PRESS

Published by Curlew Press
Derbyshire

Email: mail@curlewpress.co.uk

All rights reserved. No part of this publication may be reproduced, stored in a retrieval system or transmitted in any form or by any means, electronic, mechanical, photocopying, recording or otherwise without the prior permission of Curlew Press.

British Library Cataloguing in Publication Data: a catalogue record for this book is available from the British Library.

1st Edition

ISBN: 978-1-9161044-3-3

Print – Short Run Press Ltd.

Text – Louise Maskill

Walks – Mark Titterton

Proofreader – Ian Howe

Design and layout – Mark Titterton

Photographs – Karl Barton – front cover and p.58. All other photography by Mark Titterton.

Archive Photographs – Castleton Historical Society – p.8, p.10 both and p.19.
Curlew Press Collection – all others.

Maps – © OpenStreetMap Contributors (openstreetmap.org)

Cover – Bamford Mill, Bamford

Contents

Souvenir and Walker's Guide to the Hope Valley	4
Introduction	4
Castleton	6
Derbyshire Blue John	12
Castleton's Garland Day	14
Walk 1: Mam Tor and the Great Ridge	15
Walk 2: Castleton, the Blue John Caverns and Winnats Pass	19
Edale	23
Walk 3: Edale and the Kinder Plateau	25
Hope	29
Well dressings	30
Bradwell and Brough	31
Navio Roman fort	35
Walk 4: Hope and Bradwell	36
Bamford	42
Walk 5: Bamford and Ladybower Reservoir	46
Hathersage	49
Charlotte Brontë and Jane Eyre	53
Walk 6: Hathersage and Stanage Edge	54
Grindleford, Padley and Longshaw	58
Walk 7: Grindleford Station, Padley Gorge and Longshaw Estate	60
Bibliography	64

Souvenir and Walker's Guide to the Hope Valley

Introduction

The Hope Valley is a rural area in north Derbyshire, falling within the Peak District National Park. It follows the course of the Peakshole Water that emerges from the Peak Cavern near Castleton, joining the River Noe that has come from Edale and finally the River Derwent as they flow through Hope, Bradwell, Brough, Bamford, and Hathersage and Grindleford at the eastern end of the valley.

The valley is characterised by a broad riverside area surrounded by gritstone moorlands at the eastern end and steep limestone cliffs at the south-west, once underwater coral reefs that were exposed after millennia of erosion of the sandstone and millstone grit laid down on top of the corals. It has provided a hospitable environment for habitation for thousands of years, with evidence for settlement going back as far as the Neolithic.

The mighty Mam Tor, rising to 1,696 feet (517 metres) above sea level and overlooking the valley from the west, stands at the boundary between the sandstone Dark Peak and the limestone White Peak. Its name is Celtic, meaning 'mother mountain', but it is also known as the Shivering Mountain because of its frequent landslips caused by unstable shale underlying sandstone. The landslip on the south-eastern side is the largest active slip in the UK, and was responsible for the repeated destruction of the 'New Road' turnpike route that was eventually closed in 1979 after many attempts at repair. It is currently moving at an average annual rate of around 25 cm, although this can increase dramatically after months of heavy rainfall.

The Peak District National Park was created in 1951, the first in the UK, covering 555 square miles (1,440 km^2) and now extending into Derbyshire, Staffordshire, Cheshire, Greater Manchester and South and West Yorkshire. The Peak District's name comes not from the many hills in the area (in fact most of these are rounded, with few real peaks or summits), but from the Pecsætan, an Anglo-Saxon tribe who displaced the native Brigantes from Derbyshire and South Yorkshire after the Romans left. The Pecsætan ('peak-dwellers') settled in the central and northern parts of the Peak District and likely had farms and homesteads along the valley.

INTRODUCTION

The Great Ridge, Castleton

The Hope Valley anciently fell within the bounds of the Royal Forest of the High Peak, a royal hunting preserve administered by a High Steward based at Peveril (or Peak) Castle, above Castleton. The preserve once encompassed the parishes of Castleton, Hope, Glossop and Mottram in Cheshire and was known for its wild animals, particularly wolves. Despite draconian protection laws and heavy fines for offenders, however, the lands of the hunting preserve were gradually enclosed for agriculture or the building of houses, resulting in the landscape we see today.

The area has also been shaped by industry, notably lead mining, quarrying, and textile and corn mills powered by the many watercourses flowing down from the High Peak. The Rivers Noe and Derwent were both used for industry, with many of the villages in the Hope Valley possessing at least one mill building.

This book will visit all the most significant settlements in the Hope Valley, providing some historical background and points of interest before taking you on carefully researched guided walks so you can experience this beautiful part of Derbyshire for yourself.

The eastern face of Mam Tor

Castleton

There has been a settlement on the site of the present-day town of Castleton for millennia. Neolithic remains found in caves in Cave Dale – animal and human bones, pot sherds, flint scrapers and axes – provide evidence of continuous habitation through the Bronze and Iron Ages; indeed, there are reports of people residing in the caves right up to the 18th century.

The impressive Iron Age hillfort on the summit of Mam Tor is the largest in Derbyshire and once contained a number of huts as well as two bowl barrows. The tribe who most likely built the hillfort were the Brigantes, who were among the most powerful tribes in Britain at the time of the Roman invasion in AD 43. Castleton was certainly known to the Romans; they would have been aware of the encampment on Mam Tor, and they may have mined for lead in Odin Mine (although evidence for this is disputed).

The first written reference to Castleton (meaning 'farmstead by the castle') is in the Domesday Book of 1086, which also mentioned the first known named residents of the area, the Saxon thanes Gernebern and Hundinc. These two men held land on the estates of the Norman nobleman William Peveril, who was granted most of Derbyshire and Nottinghamshire as his demesne.

William built Peveril Castle high on a rocky eminence above Cave Dale as a seat of governance for his new estates, and Castleton grew up around it, arranged around a marketplace and enclosed by a defensive ditch. The castle was built for strength and defence, although it was also comfortable and played host to many royal and noble personages in its heyday.

The Peverils fell from grace during the 12th century, and Peveril Castle had a number of owners before passing to the Crown in 1223 and eventually to John of Gaunt (a son of Edward III) around 1359. Among John's several castles, Peveril was unimportant and isolated; in 1376 he ordered the lead to be stripped from its roofs, and by 1561 it was in a state of decay. Since then it has been mined for stone by the local residents, and even used to house animals. Today it is protected by English Heritage and is a scheduled monument.

Much of Castleton's layout dates from the Middle Ages, and some early buildings (known as cruck houses) still survive, for example on Cross Street and Back Street. Castleton Hall, close by the market square, may date back as far as the 13th century and was owned in the 17th century by Robert Ashton. The How Ashton family were Squires of Castleton and significant local landowners, later moving to Cryer House in the town. Robert's son, also Robert, invested heavily in lead mining, with shares in Odin Mine, a smelting site at Marsh Farm and a lead mill at Brough.

A later Ashton generation, Robert How Ashton, built Losehill Hall and moved there from Cryer House in 1885. Robert was a magistrate, a county councillor and an alderman, and was also a church warden who taught in the Sunday School for 25 years; by the time of his death in 1922 the Losehill estate ran to 1.5 million acres. Meanwhile the family's original home, Castleton Hall, passed through a number of hands before eventually being purchased by the Youth Hostels Association in 1943. The YHA sold the property in 1993, also relocating to Losehill Hall.

Goosehill Bridge, Castleton village

Castleton's church dates from the 12th century, with the earliest building constructed around 1100 to serve the retainers at Peveril Castle. It was originally known as the Church of Peak Castle, but in the late 14th century it was dedicated to St Edmund. The church tower was added in the late 15th century and the south porch and vestry in the early 19th century, but Norman architecture can still be seen, particularly an arch between the nave and the chancel.

Historically, transport around the Peak District was difficult; early maps show precious few roads, with people getting around on foot or horseback along ancient paths. Goods transport was via packhorse, since the challenging terrain did not allow for carts or other wheeled vehicles over long distances. However, Castleton lay at a crossroads of a number of ancient routes, and transport around the town gradually improved, especially after the Turnpike Acts of the 18th century. The road from Chapel-en-le-Frith that descends through Winnats Pass was turnpiked in 1758, and a new road below Mam Tor was built in 1811; this remained in use until 1979.

The road through Winnats Pass is very ancient, forming part of the old packhorse network. The pass is thought to be named for 'wind gates', because of the wind that blows almost incessantly through the gorge. In the mid-18th century it was the site of an infamous murder, of a young couple who were on their way to be married in the church at Peak Forest,

A group of miners photographed with human bones discovered while digging for fluorspar on Treak Cliff in 1923. Expert examination later established that this was a late Neolithic family burial about 5,500 years old.

Peak Cavern, Castleton

where marriages could be performed without the usual banns or restrictions – the 'Gretna Green of the Peak'. The couple stopped for refreshment in Castleton, but were murdered by a group of local miners as they rode up Winnats Pass and their bodies were thrown into the Speedwell Mine. No one was ever convicted of the murders, but local legend states that bad luck followed the assailants; two died in bloody accidents, one killed himself, one went mad and the last was driven by guilt to confess on his deathbed.

There has been lead-mining activity in the Castleton area since pre-Roman times. Odin Mine has been worked continuously for centuries, with ore extraction of up to 800 tonnes per annum during the 18th century. Production continued until the mine was closed down in 1869, with brief restarts in 1908 and 1909 for the extraction of fluorspar and barytes. Three of Castleton's four show caves are disused lead mines; in Speedwell Cavern visitors can take a boat journey along an underground canal. Blue John Cavern and Treak Cliff Cavern were also mined for lead as well as for the famous Derbyshire Blue John (see box).

The Peak Cavern show cave is the only natural cave system with no mining activity; its large entrance (the largest in the British Isles) was used for rope-making up to the early years of the 20th century. It is also known as the Devil's Arse; local legend states that Old Nick visits the cave to seek shelter when it rains, the Peakshole Water that issues from the cave is said to be created as he relieves himself, while the wind in the cave is his flatulence. The cave's name was changed from the Devil's Arse to the Peak Cavern to avoid offending the sensibilities of Queen Victoria when she visited in 1880 for a concert.

Left: Blacksmith's workshop, Spital Bridge, Castleton **Right:** The Peak Hotel, Castleton

Other early industries in Castleton included corn milling; a water-powered corn mill on Mill Lane was recorded as early as 1472. Lime burning for agricultural use took place at Pindale, while cotton spinning and weaving existed on a domestic scale as far back as 1648, with larger mills evolving out of the old cottage industry. There were water-powered textile mills in Castleton at Spital Bridge, at Millbridge and possibly near Peak Cavern; this one was described in 1819 and 1841 as a 'weaving shop'.

There were a good number of pubs and inns in Castleton, frequented by miners, farmers and travellers. Inns offered accommodation and stabling; the Castle Inn or Hotel is one of the oldest, in operation since the reign of Charles II. Other inns in Castleton included the George (built in 1543), the Ship and the Bull's Head. There were also private alehouses, where homeowners brewed and sold ale from their domestic dwellings. The Navigation or Speedwell was at the foot of Winnats Pass, while the Cheshire Cheese dates from 1660. Others included the Wagon and Horses, the Hart, Cave End Ale House in Cave Dale, the Brew House on Lunnons Back, the Hole in the Wall (by the south gate of the church) and the Blackrabbit (in Pindale, a well-known haunt of lead miners).

Life in Castleton today is largely based around agriculture and the tourist trade, attracting visitors to the four show caves and the natural beauty of the surrounding area. Castleton Museum is in the village's recently refurbished Visitor Centre, housing collections related to the archaeology, geology, industry, inhabitants and historical significance of the settlement – well worth a visit!

Treak Cliff Cavern

A vein of Blue John in Treak Cliff Cavern

Derbyshire Blue John

Blue John, or Derbyshire Spar, is a variety of fluorspar that is coloured blue or purple with clear or white bands, found only in the Blue John and Treak Cliff caverns in Castleton. The stone is formed when mineral solutions crystallise on the walls of voids in the surrounding limestone; eventually the crystal deposits fill the voids, with different colours reflecting variations in the chemical composition of the minerals. Blue John's characteristic blue, purple and white/clear banding is caused partly by background radiation in the surrounding rocks, as well as by iron leaching out of nearby shale beds.

Blue John has been used as a semi-precious ornamental stone for many centuries; the earliest records of Derbyshire's 'azure spar' date from the end of the 17th century. Mining the stone is a delicate business; explosives cannot be used, because they will shatter the mineral formations. Instead the surrounding rock is carefully chipped, sawn or drilled away, extracting the fragile mineral nodules whole. Current annual production is less than a tonne, although it rose as high as 20 tonnes per annum during the 18th century.

A local industry grew up in the second half of the 18th century making ornaments and jewellery for the increasing numbers of visitors to the area. Among other things, Blue John was made into vases, goblets, bowls, jewellery, salt cellars, candlesticks, obelisks, paperweights, ashtrays, knife handles, decorative eggs and doorknobs. These souvenirs were sold in Castleton and also in Matlock Bath and Buxton, taking advantage of the new fashion for health tourism centred around Derbyshire's spa waters (see *The Spa Waters of Derbyshire* by Louise Maskill, also published by Curlew Press). Fireplaces were also decorated with Blue John, commonly in surrounds or decorative plaques. Inlaying was popular in the 19th century, with carefully shaped pieces of Blue John forming designs set into larger items; tables, church screens and fireplaces all featured this type of work.

The working of Blue John today centres on Castleton, in a select number of workshops. Vases, bowls and goblets are usually worked from chunks of Blue John, carefully chosen so that the natural colour banding runs parallel to the rim of the item. Rings, brooches and beads are made from mineral slices. The stone does not sparkle in the same way as other gemstones, so it is rarely faceted; instead, items are polished to a shine, and are usually made sufficiently thin that light can pass through them and reveal the colours and structure of the stone.

Above: Extracting Blue John with a diamond tipped chainsaw, Treak Cliff Cavern

Left: A Blue John urn

The Garland King outside *The George* pub

Castleton's Garland Day

Castleton is known for its unique celebration of Oak Apple Day on 29 May. The date commemorates the restoration of the English monarchy in May 1660, but in Castleton the day is marked by a unique ceremony known as Garlanding – although some believe that the custom of making floral decorations and offering them to local deities goes back much further than the 17th century, perhaps as far as the Celtic Iron Age.

In Castleton, around 29 May a large wooden frame is decorated with leaves and flowers topped by a smaller garland or posy (known as the 'queen'). The whole thing is worn by a 'king', covering him from the waist upwards. He and his consort then parade on horseback through the village, stopping at various places (including all six of the pubs) and accompanied by the Castleton Silver Band and schoolchildren dressed in white, who dance a form of Morris at each stop.

The parade ends at the church gates, where the small garland is removed to be placed on the village war memorial. The larger frame is hoisted to the top of the church steeple and placed atop the central pinnacle, where it remains for the rest of the week (in former times it was left until it had disintegrated). The day concludes with maypole dancing in the marketplace, and a dancing parade through the village with the residents dancing the 'criss cross' to the village band.

Walk 1: Mam Tor and the Great Ridge

Essential Information

Distance and Approximate Walking Time: 6 miles, 3–3½ hours

Parking: Old Mam Tor Road, take the turn off the main road signed to the Blue John Cavern. Near Mam Tor, Castleton

Start: Old Mam Tor Road/Blue John Cavern entrance

About the Walk

From the Old Mam Tor Road near the entrance to the Blue John Cavern we take the footpath to the summit of Mam Tor, also known as Shivering Mountain or the Mother Hill. This imposing eminence sits on the Great Ridge at almost 1,700 feet (517 metres) above sea level. Mam Tor was the site of a Bronze and Iron Age hillfort; our walk takes in the original inturned entrances in the earthen ramparts at the western (below the summit) and eastern ends of the hillfort.

We walk along the Great Ridge path, which extends 2 miles from Mam Tor to Lose Hill via Hollins Cross and Back Tor. There are spectacular views to our left over the Vale of Edale and the northern gritstone moors, and to our right over the Hope Valley and limestone plateau. We return via the footpath, traversing the hillside below the ridgeway path that we followed on the outward leg of the walk.

Finally, after descending the ridge we climb the Old Mam Tor Road (known locally as 'New Road') back towards the Blue John Cavern. This section of road was constructed by the Sheffield and Chapel-en-le-Frith Turnpike Company in the early 19th century to replace the packhorse route up the steeper gradient of Winnats Pass. However, it suffered a series of landslides throughout the 20th century and was in constant need of repair and maintenance; it was eventually abandoned and permanently closed to traffic in 1979 after a massive landslip from the side of Shivering Mountain, and traffic was rerouted back through Winnats Pass.

The abandoned road below Mam Tor

Directions

1. Start on the Old Mam Tor Road at the end of the driveway to the Blue John Cavern. Walk up the road towards the junction with the main road. Take the footpath on the right, about 100 yards before the road junction.

2. Follow the footpath up the open access land to a gate and walk up some steps to reach the Edale Road. Turn up the road, and after a few yards take the footpath on the right to Mam Tor.

3. Climb the steps and flagstone footpath to the trig point on the summit of Mam Tor.

4. Continue on the flagstone footpath along the Great Ridge for just under a mile to reach Hollins Cross. Paths join the ridge here from both the Vale of Edale and the Hope Valley. A memorial to walker Tom Hyett stands where a cross was once raised.

5. Follow the path that ascends steadily away from Hollins Cross along the ridge. After about half a mile where a path joins

WALK 1: MAM TOR AND THE GREAT RIDGE

the ridge from the Hope Valley side, we go through a gate in the fence on the left and continue on the path that climbs up onto Back Tor.

6. From the summit of Back Tor, walk another half mile along the ridge path to Lose Hill. We pass several cairns (large piles of stones) along the way, and there is a gentle climb and a stone viewpoint marker on the summit.

7. Stay on the flagstone path going away from the viewpoint that descends into the Hope Valley. After about 350 yards go over a stile and walk to another stile in the fence on the right prior to a cairn. Go over this stile and take the path ahead to traverse the valley side.

8. Follow the partially waymarked footpath to Brockett Booth Plantation. Go through a gate and walk through the plantation, exiting via a gate on the opposite side.

9. Keep to the path ahead, which traverses below and adjacent to the

On the Great Ridge looking towards Mam Tor

ridgeway path that we walked earlier. At a waymarker continue straight ahead (do not descend). As we make our way further along the path there are some wooden posts with waymarkers attached. Follow this path to rejoin the Great Ridge at Hollins Cross, which we passed earlier.

10. Go through the gate to the memorial stone marking Hollins Cross and take the gate immediately on the left, make sure you keep to the right fork in the path towards Mam Tor as you begin to descend.

11. At a fork in the path just after some upright standing stones on the right, stay to the right (do not descend). The path skirts around the perimeter of the wood and follows the contours of the hillside to the abandoned Old Mam Tor Road.

12. At the road, turn right and walk up to a gate and bus turning area. It is just a short distance up the road to the end of the walk near the bus stop and the entrance to Blue John Cavern.

Walk 2: Castleton, the Blue John Caverns and Winnats Pass

Essential Information

Distance and Approximate Walking Time: 4½ miles, 1½–2 hours

Parking: Castleton Car Park, Cross Street, Castleton, S33 8WH (fees applicable)

Start: Peak District National Park Visitor Centre, Castleton

About the Walk

Castleton lies at the western end of the Hope Valley, and is home to the Blue John Cavern and other show caves for which it is perhaps best known. Our walk commences at the Peak District National Park Visitor Centre in the village, where you will find a shop, a café and a small museum managed by the Castleton Historical Society – well worth a visit.

We walk towards the head of the valley, taking to the fields on the footpath criss-crossing Odin Sitch on our way to the former lead ore workings at Odin Mine in the shadow of Mam Tor. We pass the surviving crushing circle with its gritstone wheel, surrounded by old spoil heaps that now support a variety of plant species including the common spotted orchid. The mine workings extend westward across the old road for approximately a kilometre. (**Note**: Do not enter any of the old mine workings; they contain deep shafts, and the tunnels are dangerous and prone to collapse.)

Winnats Pass

19

After following the Old Mam Tor Road for a short distance, we take a path on the right that climbs and traverses over Treak Cliff Hill, passing the entrances to the Treak Cliff and Blue John Caverns along the way. Below our feet is a subterranean network of passages and natural caves that were enlarged by miners while extracting Blue John. A series of New Caves adorned with stalactites were discovered at the Treak Cliff Cavern by spa miners in 1926, opening to visitors in the 1930s.

We return to Castleton following the path down the spectacular Winnats Pass. This deep dry gorge was first formed in the Carboniferous period as a channel between reefs in a shallow lagoon. Later it filled up with shales (which became gritstone) as the delta spread into the sea, and later still it was re-excavated by the action of stream water during and after the last Ice Age. At the bottom of the pass, just after Speedwell Cavern, we take a right turn over Longcliffe back to the village. The walk concludes with a detour to St Edmund's Church before returning to the Visitor Centre.

Winnats Pass

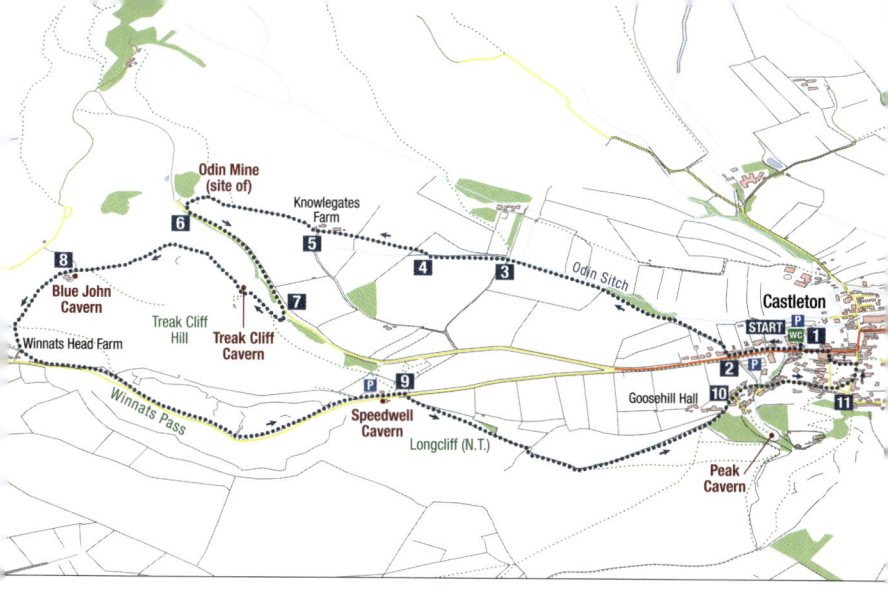

Directions

1. Outside the Peak District National Park Visitor Centre, turn right along the main road and walk along the pavement towards Treak Cliff and Speedwell Caverns. Shortly after passing the Methodist Chapel take the next public footpath on the right.

2. Once in the open field follow the path, at first keeping a stone wall on your left, to a wooden gate. Beyond the gate, continue on the path with the stream (Odin Sitch) over the stone wall to your right.

3. When you reach a narrow lane, continue on the path immediately opposite towards Mam Tor, keeping the stream to your right.

4. Just beyond a standing stone or former gatepost, cross over the stream and turn left to continue on the path a short distance to a wooden gate in the stone wall. The path continues over the field to Knowlegates Farm.

5. At the entrance to the farm, continue straight ahead on the path that skirts the boundary of the farm buildings. Ascend some steps as the path rises and continue to the site of Odin Mine (a former lead mine). Just after crossing a stream via a footbridge you will pass the ore crushing circle on your left. Climb the path to the road above.

6. Turn left and walk down the road.

7. Turn right and climb the steps to the Treak Cliff Cavern. At the entrance to the cavern, continue up the steps to the left and turn right on the footpath at the perimeter of the buildings. The path traverses Treak Cliff Hill and then climbs steadily to a private road to Blue John Cavern.

21

SOUVENIR AND WALKER'S GUIDE TO THE HOPE VALLEY

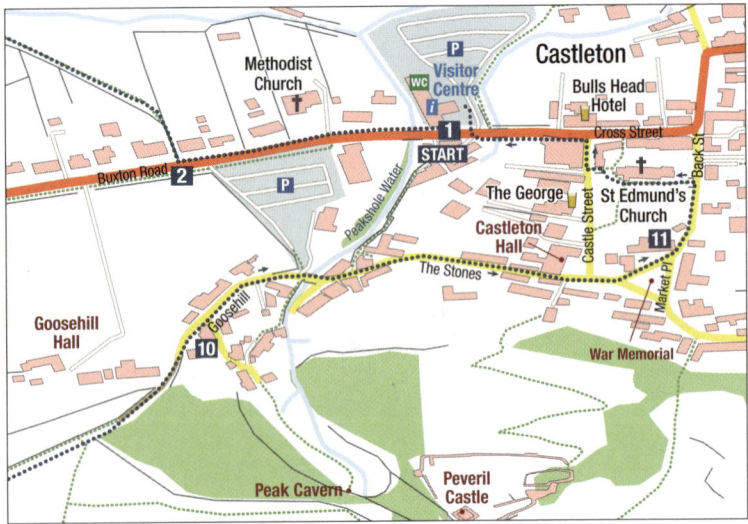

8. Pass the Blue John Cavern buildings on your left to reach a gate ahead. Continue on the path towards Winnats Head Farm. To the left of the farm is a gate in the wall leading to the road; turn left in front of the gate and follow the path down Winnats Pass to the car park at Speedwell Cavern.

9. Just beyond the car park, turn right on the footpath over Longcliffe (NT) towards Peak Cavern. Follow the path, keeping the boundary wall close on your left, back to the edge of Castleton village.

10. Follow the lane (Goosehill) down the hill, cross over the road bridge and walk up the lane (The Stones) to the Market Place (look out for the village green and war memorial).

11. Go left down Back Street, turn left into the churchyard and follow the footpath around the church to Castle Street. Turn right on Castle Street to the junction with Cross Street (the main road) and turn left to return to the Visitor Centre.

Cross Street, Castleton

Edale

Edale

The name of the village of Edale is also the name of the valley of the River Noe, wherein the village lies. From the Norman Conquest the area lay in the Royal Forest of the High Peak; the name *Aidele* is recorded in the Domesday Book of 1086. The settlement was established from the 13th century onwards, developing from a scatter of farms in the valley into a village in its own right.

The village is a common starting point for challenging walks on the high rolling moorland plateau of Kinder Scout, covered by peat bogs and cleft by deep channels that fill with water during rainy periods. The range includes the highest point in the Peak District, and was the site of the historic Kinder Trespass in April 1932, when three groups of ramblers ascended Kinder from different directions in protest against the fact that walkers were being denied access to large areas of open land in England (which were often owned and managed by wealthy landowners or the Crown). There were violent scuffles with gamekeepers on the Kinder Plateau and a number of the ramblers were arrested, but the trespass has been hailed as one of the most successful acts of civil disobedience in British history, since it arguably led to the passage of the National Parks legislation in 1949 and the creation of long-distance footpaths such as

The Vale of Edale from Edale Moor (Kinder Plateau)

the Pennine Way (which starts at the Old Nags Head pub in Edale and crosses Kinder). On a clear day the views from the plateau can include Manchester, Stockport, Warrington, Chester and the hills of North Wales.

Edale Cross is shaped of millstone grit, standing at the top of Jacob's Ladder, a well-known ascent to Kinder. It used to be known as Champion Cross, a corruption of 'Champayne', the old name for the southern area of the Peak Forest that included much open grazing land. The cross stands on the parish boundary, and is likely to have served as a territorial marker as well as a guide stone.

Holy Trinity Church in the village was completed in 1886, replacing a chapel built in 1812 which itself supplanted an earlier structure dating from 1633. The village was also the site of Cresswell's Mill, built in 1795 on the site of an earlier corn mill and tannery. Mill workers were brought in from far and wide; some were housed in cottages or a nearby accommodation block known as Skinner's Hall, but many from the local area simply walked from their homes. A large number of women made the trip daily from Castleton, walking over the thousand-foot Hollins Cross pass. The mill continued in the production of cotton until the 1940s but fell into disrepair after its closure, until restoration and conversion to residential use in the 1970s.

Walk 3: Edale and the Kinder Plateau

Essential Information

Distance and Approximate Walking Time: 7 miles, 3½–4½ hours

Parking: Edale Car Park, Water Meadows, Hope Road, Edale, S33 7ZQ (fees applicable)

Start: Edale Car Park

About the Walk

Edale railway station on the Hope Valley Line (linking Sheffield and Manchester) provides convenient and frequent access to the village. The station was opened in 1894 by the Midland Railway, and is now operated by Northern Trains and the East Midlands Railway; the typical service is hourly in both directions, making this an easy way to get to and from the village for a day's walking.

This walk begins from the main village car park, or from the station if arriving by train. We follow the lane into Edale and pick up the Pennine Way for a short distance before taking the path that climbs up to Grindslow Knoll. This is perhaps the easiest route up onto the Kinder Plateau, and the climb is well rewarded with a spectacular 360-degree panoramic view from the cairn on the summit of Grindslow Knoll.

At an elevation of 2,087 feet (636 metres) above sea level the flat-topped moorland plateau of Kinder Scout is the highest point in the Peak District. This area of the Dark Peak is characterised by its moorland, heather and dark millstone grit shales, while the Kinder Plateau is also well known for its extensive network of deep peat groughs or channels, some cutting right through to the gritstone bedrock.

We follow the path that winds around the edge of the Kinder Plateau, crossing Grindsbrook Clough and passing some fantastic naturally sculpted gritstone rocks along the way. At Golden Clough we leave the plateau, turning sharply downwards on a path that eventually brings us back to the valley bottom north of Edale. We cross the Grinds Brook one final time and climb out of the gorge to a lane on the outskirts of the village. If you are in need of some well-earned refreshment, the excellent Old Nags Head pub is just a short distance from here. Finally, retrace your footsteps from outside the pub along the level lane to the end of the walk.

Directions

1. Leave the car park on the footpath at the side of the public convenience (signed to the Moorland Centre Edale). At the bottom of the steps, cross the lane and turn right along the pavement. Pass underneath the railway bridge. If arriving by train you will join the walk at this point.

2. Walk along the road for about a third of a mile to Edale village, passing the Rambler Inn, the Moorland Centre and the church along the way. On arriving in Edale village, continue past the primary school, and just in front of the Old Nags Head pub turn left onto the footpath at a wooden fingerpost signed for the Pennine Way.

3. Continue up the track, going between the cottages and through a gate. Stay on the footpath ahead, at first with a cottage and then an old barn on your left-hand side, and continue up between the trees.

4. Where the path opens out into pasture, continue ahead towards Grindslow Knoll as indicated by the fingerpost (ignoring the 'Pennine Way' path on the left). As we begin to ascend the open pasture the path crosses a field boundary where the wall is missing; keep ahead at this point (bearing in a roughly one o'clock direction).

5. At the top of the pasture, go through the gate onto the path that climbs all the way to Grindslow Knoll (half a mile). About two thirds of the way up the path, after a gate in a boundary fence, the gradient becomes steeper. As the path nears the top, bear left to reach the cairn on the summit of

Grindslow Knoll. Enjoy the wonderful 360-degree panoramic views from this vantage point before continuing the walk.

6. From the summit cairn, take the path straight ahead that descends and follows closely around the contours of the Grindsbrook valley, with the edge dropping away sharply on your right-hand side. As you proceed there are splendid views from the path down into Grindsbrook Clough. We follow this path around the edge of the Kinder Plateau until we descend to Edale.

7. Continue on the path to a large cairn (a pile of stones) that marks the location where a tributary of the Grinds Brook spills over into Grindsbrook Clough. Pass in front of the cairn and bear right to stay on the path around the edge of the Kinder Plateau (do not descend).

8. We cross another tributary of the Grinds Brook near the head of Grindsbrook Clough, where the path dips down to cross the brook. You will see the path on the opposite side which again follows the contours around the edge of the plateau.

9. After approximately a third of a mile the path crosses another stream that spills off the edge.

10. Keep along the path for about one mile, at which point we leave the main path and turn right onto another path that descends towards a large cairn. Pass to the left of the cairn and stay on the path as it continues to descend (ignoring a path off to the left).

11. Continue along the path. At the top of a grassy knoll the path bends sharply around to the right; continue to follow the path all the way down to a gate in a high stone wall.

12. Go through the gate and walk downhill to join a flagstone path near the bottom of the valley. Turn left and follow the path, which eventually descends into woodland and to a footbridge over Grinds Brook. Cross the footbridge and climb the steps on the other side to a lane.

13. Turn left down the lane into Edale. From the centre of the village, retrace your steps past the church and the Moorland Centre to complete the walk.

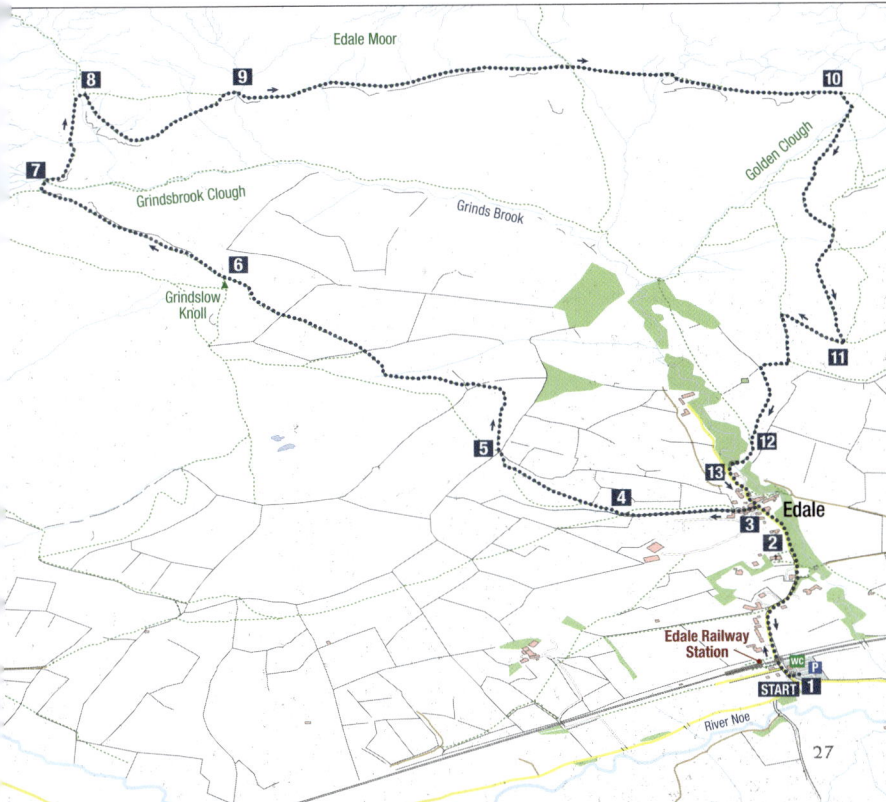

Looking across Grindslow Knoll from Edale Moor (Kinder Plateau)

Hope

The village of Hope is of great antiquity. There was prehistoric activity in the area going back as far as the Mesolithic, with active settlement stretching through the Bronze and Iron Ages. There was also intensive Roman activity at the fort of Navio at nearby Brough and the Batham Gate road leading south-west to Buxton and northeast to Templeborough Fort near Rotherham.

The seven-foot carved stem of a Saxon cross near the church provides evidence that the village was a local centre of worship and habitation going back many centuries; the village was listed as possessing a church in the Domesday Book of 1086, and the current Church of St Peter was restored and enlarged in the 14th and 15th centuries from a much earlier building. Leyland notes that although the church has no ancient monuments, it is notable for its 'strange, grotesque gargoyles'. There is also an important medieval fortification in the shape of Hope Motte, a conical flat-topped mound surrounded by a ditch that was likely once the centre of local Norman power before the focus shifted to Peveril Castle at Castleton in the 12th century.

Hope has always been an agricultural settlement, and this heritage is celebrated each year in the Hope Show. This is one of the Peak District's major summer farming shows, held over the August Bank Holiday and offering everything from livestock classes, equine events and sheepdog trials to vintage tractors and classic cars.

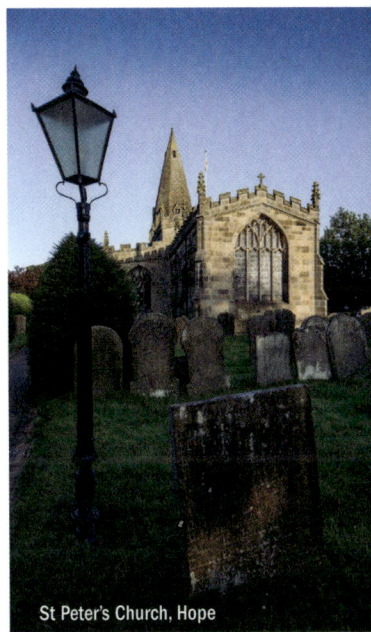
St Peter's Church, Hope

Ashton's Engine House, Pindale

Lead mining was another important industry in the area, with Ashton's Mine in Pindale at one time producing more lead than Odin Mine in Castleton. The mine's pumping engine house is still intact. More recent industry in the area may be found in the Hope Cement works, supplied by raw materials from the nearby Bradwell quarry. There has been a cement works on this site since 1929; the current Breedon plant is the largest in the UK. The Edale Mountain Rescue Team is also based here, one of the busiest teams in the country, covering parts of Derbyshire and South Yorkshire.

Well dressings

The well dressings of the Peak District attract thousands of visitors every summer. Villages across Derbyshire and Staffordshire decorate their wells, springs, fountains and other public water sources, with communities (and sometime visitors) coming together to design, create and display these ephemeral works of art. The villages of the Hope Valley are no exception.

Well dressing, St Peter's Church, Hope

The origins of the ritual are obscure, with theories ranging from pagan veneration of water deities to medieval thanksgiving ceremonies after the passing of the Black Death or other disasters. Complicated designs are transferred from paper to a specially prepared clay layer in a wooden frame, and then many hours of work and communal effort go into creating the images using natural materials such as seeds, leaves and petals.

The completed dressings are displayed around the village, often as part of a summer celebration centred around the saint's day of the local parish church. In the Hope Valley, Hathersage decorates two wells during its Gala in early July, while Hope dresses four wells during a Wakes Week in late June. The residents of Bamford decorate two wells in mid-July.

Bradwell and Brough

The name of the village of Bradwell is thought to come from Broad Wall, referring to the Roman fortifications at nearby Brough. Until relatively recently (in the early 20th century) it was known as Bradwall, although the local dialect name is 'Bradda'. It was known to the Romans; there is possible archaeological evidence of a small Romano-British settlement in Bradwell Dale, near Hazelbadge, and the Romans certainly took an interest in the local lead mines. A Roman pig of lead was found during an archaeological excavation in 1891, and it is possible that part of the duty of the nearby fort was to maintain order at the mines. Bradwell continued as a lead-mining settlement until the industry faded and died out locally.

A notable monument in the village is the Grey Ditch linear embankment and ditch, variously interpreted as a 5th–7th-century defence against Anglo-Saxon encroachment during the Viking period, or as an early medieval boundary marker across the head of the valley of the Bradwell Brook. Eden Tree, on the Roman road, was once known as Edwin's Tree and is said to be the site of a great battle during the Dark Ages, when a tribal king called Edwin was captured and hanged on a tree at this spot.

Hazelbadge Hall stands at the head of Bradwell Dale. The Hazelbadge estate came into the hands of the Strelley family around 1154, when the Peverils of Castleton fell from power. A manor was originally built on the hall site by the Strelleys, but that has long since gone; the present buildings were built in 1549 and bear the arms of the Vernon family of Haddon, who acquired the estate in 1421. The house has a long and impressive history; as well as being the home of the Vernon family for many generations, it was also a royal shooting lodge and a seat of judgement, with courts held here by the High Steward of the Forest.

The area also has a ghost. The story goes that Margaret Vernon, among the last of the Vernons to live at Hazelbadge before it passed to the Manners family in the late 16th century, fell in love with a local man. However, he was already betrothed to another, and on discovering his treachery she vowed to witness his marriage in Hope Church. Afterwards she was so distraught that she rode for home as if pursued by the devil himself, and the shock and emotional upset brought on a fatal fever. On wild and stormy nights her ghost is still said to gallop between Hope and Hazelbadge on a spectral steed.

For many centuries there was no Anglican church in Bradwell; villagers worshipped at the parish church of St Peter in Hope. However, there were Nonconformists in the village from the start of the movement in the

Hazelbadge Hall, Bradwell Dale

17th century, and a Presbyterian chapel was built in Bradwell in 1662, the first public place of worship in the village. At that time dissension was a crime and Nonconformist worshippers were persecuted and sometimes even martyred.

Methodism in Bradwell also dates back almost to the beginning of that movement; a number of village families were active, and John Wesley, the founder of Methodism, preached in the village in 1747 and 1765. The Methodists held meetings in barns and rooms in private dwellings until the first chapel was built in 1768 on Fern Bank. Another Wesleyan Chapel was built in 1807, a first Primitive Methodist Chapel in 1823 followed by a second in 1845, and a Baptist Chapel was opened in the latter years of 18th century.

Eventually the Anglican St Barnabas' Church was built in 1868 as a chapel of ease for the mother church in Hope, although Bradwell remained part of the Hope parish until 1875 when a new parish was endowed, centred on Bradwell and including Hazelbadge, Great Hucklow, Little Hucklow, Abney, Grindlow and Wardlow.

For many centuries lead mining was the main industry in the area. Whole families shared the labour, with men and boys toiling in the mines and smelting mills while women, girls and younger children processed the ore. Wages were very low and mining families were affected by the poisonous effects of the ore, frequently suffering crippling poverty, chronic ill health and early death. Lead mining as a domestic industry declined in the first half of the 19th century, with small mines no longer viable or profitable in competition with bigger, more technologically advanced outfits.

Lead mining was a dangerous trade. In 1854 there was a disaster in the slag works at Dale End in Bradwell, when two miners, William Mitchell and Joseph Hallam, were suffocated by sulphurous fumes while trying to vent the mine, and two more men, John Edwy Darnley and Jonah Elliott, lost their lives trying to save them. There were miraculous escapes, though. In 1715 John Frost was buried in a mine at Hucklow when the ceiling caved in; digging him out took upwards of seventy hours because the rescuers had to proceed with extreme care to avoid further collapse. John was eventually extracted with no more than bruises and a broken leg, having passed the time by singing hymns and psalms.

Bradwell

Weaving was also a cottage industry before the Industrial Revolution, and many households in Bradwell had looms. There was a silk mill at the bottom of Water Lane, a cotton mill by the brook at Eden Tree, and another at Brough which was later converted into a lead works. Hat-making was carried out in Bradwell for many years, with several small workshops producing the felt hats worn by miners and known as Bradda hats, for the name of the village. The Middleton and Evans families were particularly known for this trade; Job Middleton was the last known manufacturer, dying in 1899 aged 85.

Samuel Fox (1815–1887) lived in a small house in Water Lane (now Church Street). He served his apprenticeship in the wire trade in Hathersage and Sheffield, and then set up his own wire business in Stocksbridge, Yorkshire. He invented the 'Paragon' steel umbrella frame in 1851, but his business also diversified into crucible steel, rails and rods. Fox remained very attached to Bradwell throughout his life and was a regular visitor and benefactor, although these gifts were always anonymous. It was only a few years before his death that his identity as a donor became public; in his will he bequeathed a sum of £1,000 to the village, with the interest to go to the poor of Bradwell in perpetuity. The Samuel Fox Country Inn in the village is named in his honour.

Today, Bradwell is known far and wide for the excellent Bradwell's Ice Cream, with a wide range of flavours produced in the village for over a century and served in cafés, restaurants and parks across the area, as well as in regional supermarkets and independent stores. Watch out for it as you explore the Peak District!

Bradwell, c.1900

Navio Roman fort

The Roman fort at Navio (Brough) was built around AD 75–80 under the governorship of Agricola, part of the legions' push northwards to subdue the Brigantes. Roads linking settlements and forts across the Peaks and Yorkshire formed a complex supply chain, and allowed Agricola to sweep further northwards and establish a frontier with Scotland by AD 80. Navio was at a junction of three Roman roads – Batham Gate south to Buxton (Aquae Arnemetiae) and the baths there, Doctor's Gate north-west to the Melandra fort near Glossop, and the Long Causeway north-east to Sheffield. This would have meant that Navio, and the associated settlement at Bradwell, were of some importance to the occupying forces.

The fort was sited on the River Noe, close to its confluence with the Bradwell Brook, and once encompassed an area of 2.5 acres. It boasted defensive walls six feet thick, four gateways, and a turret or tower at each corner. Buildings inside the complex included a central HQ and a probable bath house. A 1903 excavation found a masonry pit or vault some eight feet deep containing fragments of inscribed stone commemorating the Emperor Pius (AD 138–161) and the First Aquitani Cohort, who presumably garrisoned the fort at the time. Coins, pottery, bones and an altar stone were also found.

Much of the stone foundations of the fort remains below ground, and above ground some earthworks still survive. Near the centre of the scheduled monument there are some dressed gritstone slabs which show diamond broaching, a technique favoured by the Romans to dress worked building stone. Finds from excavations at Navio are displayed in Buxton Museum, and ploughing and building work in the fields and surrounding area have produced much evidence of extensive and lengthy Roman activity in the locality, notably a vicus (settlement) adjoining the fort. Stone buildings and walls in the nearby hamlet of Brough contain a number of Roman incised or worked stones, and it is thought locally that stone from the fort may also have been used in the construction of the earliest church at Hope.

Walk 4: Hope and Bradwell

Essential Information

Distance and Approximate Walking Time: 8 miles, 4–5 hours

Parking: Hope Car Park, Hope, S33 6RS (fees applicable)

Start: Hope Car Park

About the Walk

This longer walk takes in the villages of Hope and Bradwell as well as the hamlet of Brough. There are many interesting features along the way including the Navio Roman fort and the Grey Ditch, an early medieval earthwork embankment thought to have been a boundary marker or a defensive structure.

Roman masonry, Navio Fort

Starting in Hope, we leave the village and follow the banks of the River Noe. After a section of raised pavement along the road the path crosses a field to the hamlet of Brough, where we pass the former corn mill beside its weir, which can be observed from the footbridge. From Brough we make our way over the fields to Bradwell, and as we near the village the path crosses the Grey Ditch for the first time.

We leave the village to climb Bradwell Edge, taking the time to look back and admire the views across the Hope Valley stretching all the way to Mam Tor and beyond on a clear day. We return to Brough via Brough Lane; the track crosses the eastern terminal of the Grey Ditch before descending into the valley. It is just a short distance from Brough to the Navio Roman fort; the path goes straight through the site of the fort. Look out for the surviving earthworks and dressed stones.

Finally we return through open pastureland and along the lane to St Peter's Church in Hope. The church dates to the 14th century; there is an Anglo-Saxon cross shaft in the churchyard, and the grotesque stone carvings on the waterspouts of the church are an interesting feature worth seeking out. See how many you can spot!

Bradwell from Bradwell Edge

Directions

1. Leave the car park and cross Castleton Road (A6187) via the pedestrian crossing. Turn right and walk along the pavement towards the church.

2. Just prior to the Old Hall Hotel, take a left turn into Edale Road.

3. Continue along the road for about 400 yards, then take a right turn down Bowden Lane.

4. Just after the narrow road bridge spanning the River Noe, take the footpath on the right. With the river on your right, follow the track to its end, passing a dwelling on your left that was formerly a corn mill. Just in front of a stone wall, turn left up some stone steps to a gate, then go right to continue on the footpath. The path follows the course of the river (ignore a left turn after a gate) to reach some steps leading to Hope Road (A6187).

5. Cross the road to the pavement opposite, turn left and walk for approximately 325 yards to the turning for Hope Station. The pavement ends here on this side of the road, so cross carefully and continue along Hope Road on the pavement opposite. Pass Laneside Farm on your right and another building behind a stone wall on the left, prior to where the road bends to the left. Just beyond the bend, where it is safe to do so, cross the road with care to take the footpath on the right, passing through a narrow gap in the hedge and over a stile into the field beyond.

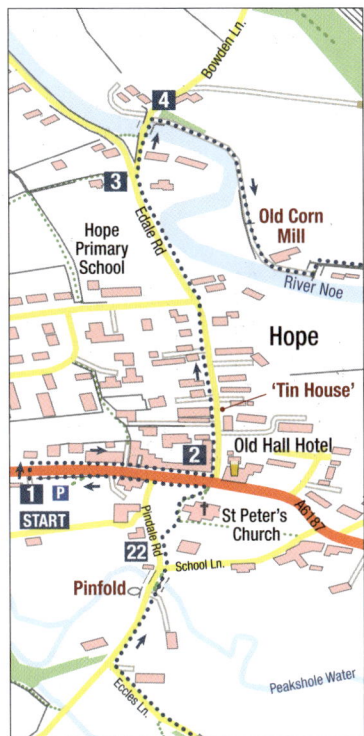

6. Bear to the left after the stile and walk diagonally across the field. The path clips the trees to your right and continues across the field to a gate by the side of a small Severn Trent building and to the road.

7. Turn right along the road towards Brough, crossing the river via a modern footbridge adjacent to the road. On your right is Brough Corn Mill, home to the agricultural merchants William Eyre and Sons.

8. Continue past the mill and take the next left turn into Brough Lane. Walk a few yards up the lane and turn right up the

Left: Bessie Lane, Bradwell **Right:** Soft Water Lane, Bradwell

track at the side of some ruined buildings. The track bears left in front of a garage building. Go through a gate and keep the trees and boundary on your right; at the end of a tall metal fence just in front of a ramshackle barn, turn left up the field towards a couple of half-fallen stone posts and turn right to continue along the path.

9. Follow this path for about a mile to Bradwell, keeping in the same general direction over numerous fields and stiles. On our way we follow overhead power lines for a while, cross two farm tracks and a further three fields.

10. After negotiating a stile and five small square stepping stones we reach the Grey Ditch. The medieval frontier or defensive boundary is now a fairly indistinct shallow bank about a metre high and seven metres wide, with a corresponding ditch around 3 feet deep and 16 feet wide; the footpath cuts across the site. Continue over the final series of fields to Soft Water Lane in Bradwell.

11. Go straight ahead along the lane to the junction with Church Street (B6049). Turn left at the traffic lights along Church Street. Pass St Barnabas' Church and the Shoulder of Mutton.

12. Stay on the pavement as it bears left by the metal railings in front of some cottages (away from the B6049). The path passes up a channel between two cottages and ascends some stone steps.

13. Continue ahead up the lane and take the narrow lane straight ahead; note a sign on the cottage for Bessie Lane. Keep left on this lane as it drops downhill. Just after some garages or workshops on the left where the lane splits, take the right fork up Edge Lane, ascending to Edge Cottage and the footpath onto Bradwell Edge.

14. Go through the gate and climb the path straight ahead, keeping the boundary close on your right. At a small standing stone or waymarker, continue on the main path for another 25 yards and then turn right.

15. Follow this path to the top of the edge where there is a drystone wall directly in front, and go through a squeeze stile to the field beyond. Follow the path over two fields to Brough Lane (track).

16. Turn left along the lane.

17. After about half a mile, just beyond the point where a footpath joins on the left, the lane truncates the eastern end of the Grey Ditch. This is the best-preserved section of the medieval earthwork, where it defended the ridge north of Rebellion Knoll. Continue down Brough Lane past a private entrance and road to Elmore Hill Farm; here the track becomes a sealed road. Follow this road without deviation all the way down to the junction with the main road in Brough.

18. Cross the road (B6049) with care to the pavement opposite and turn left. Go over the footbridge alongside the road bridge and through the gate on the right, signed to Hope and Castleton via the 'Roman Station Anavio'.

19. The path passes between two wooden gateposts at the side of an old ladder stile. We are now on the site of the Navio Roman fort (see feature box on page 35 for further information). A pile of worked Roman stones sit on the ground to the left of the footpath.

20. Continue ahead towards the trees to a footbridge, and then follow the fence along the field boundary. Negotiate the next stile and continue following the fence and boundary for about another 350 yards, then bear right down the grassy holloway or track to a gate (opening) in the stone wall. Go through here and follow the path to a metal gate and a stile.

21. Turn right down Eccles Lane. At the end of the lane, turn right down Pindale Road. Look out for the pinfold (an animal shelter or pound) on the opposite side of the road just before the road bridge. Cross the footbridge at the side of the road bridge.

22. At the edge of the church boundary wall, take the footpath on the right leading to the churchyard. Take some time to look around the church, and then exit the churchyard down the stone steps through the gate (opposite the Old Hall Hotel) and turn left to return along the road back to the car park.

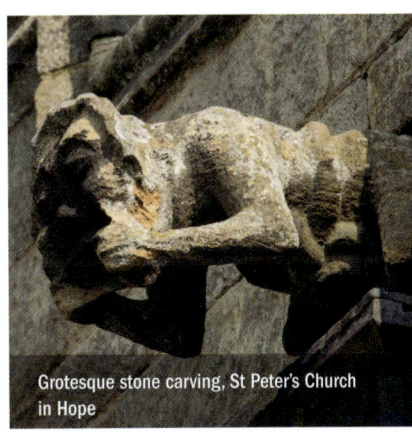

Grotesque stone carving, St Peter's Church in Hope

Bamford Mill

Bamford

Bamford was recorded in the Domesday Book as *Banford*, a settlement with only eight villagers and two smallholders (likely just a pair of households). By 1086 the area had been granted to Ralph Fitzhubert, Baron of Crich, a Norman lord who had become a major landowner across Derbyshire and Nottinghamshire.

Bamford developed around its mill, which predates the Industrial Revolution. A water-powered corn mill was built here in the 1780s, later converted to a cotton mill after it was damaged by fire. It was a busy enterprise, employing around 230 people by the 1850s and continuing in operation until it was acquired by Courtaulds in 1963, eventually closing in 1965. The building saw different industrial uses before being converted to private apartments in the 1990s; the mill engine, dating from 1907 and named *Edna*, is preserved onsite, although she is not operational at present.

The village is close to the Ladybower, Derwent and Howden Reservoirs, and it was in Bamford, in the graveyard of the Church of St John the Baptist, that some burials from the drowned villages of Ashopton and Derwent were reinterred. These small settlements were both evacuated, dismantled and submerged when this stretch of the Upper Derwent Valley was flooded by the Derwent Valley Water Board in the early 1940s, creating the three reservoirs to supply the industrial cities of Derby, Nottingham, Leicester and Sheffield. The two villages are both under Ladybower; Ashopton, close to the present viaduct carrying the A57 road over the mouth of the Derwent Valley, is covered in a thick layer of silt, but the ruins of Derwent are still occasionally visible when water levels drop – most recently in the summer of 2018.

Although most of the buildings were dismantled, the spire of Derwent's chapel of St James was initially left standing as a memorial to the two lost villages. It did eventually disappear from view under the water, but remerged periodically when the water level was low. However, it was finally demolished in 1947 because of safety concerns. Another significant building to be lost was Derwent Hall, originally a much older farmhouse that was acquired in 1672 by the Balguy family and converted into an elegant residence later owned by the Duke of Norfolk. It had extensive ornamental grounds and (ironically) a lake, and contained a remarkable collection of early wood panels and carvings and panelling; these were

The lost village of Ashopton

mostly salvaged when the hall was dismantled in 1943. A 'peeping Tom' stone carving from the stables may now be seen at Losehill Hall YHA.

Near Bamford is the site of the temporary hamlet of Birchinlee, known locally as 'Tin Town'. It was occupied between 1902 and 1916 by construction workers who were employed to build the Derwent and Howden dams, along with their families. Birchinlee had medical facilities, a school, shops, a post office, a police station, a railway station and much else. The population rose as high as 900 people living in well-constructed huts; one of these was salvaged and can be seen on Edale Road in Hope. The remains of the village can be seen from footpaths on the west of Derwent Reservoir.

One significant part of Derwent's architectural history to be saved from the flooding of Ladybower was the packhorse bridge that once carried travellers across the River Derwent. Dating from 1672 and originally sited near Derwent Hall, it was dismantled and eventually rebuilt in 1959 at the head of Howden Reservoir near the former ford site of Slippery Stones. It now spans the Derbyshire–Yorkshire border and carries a bridleway.

The best-known period of Derwent Reservoir's history must surely be its use in World War 2 as an operational test site for the famous bouncing bombs developed by Barnes Wallis to attack German dams in the Ruhr Valley. Wallis was a local boy, born in Ripley, Derbyshire in 1887, and during the war he recognised a need for the strategic bombing of military, civil engineering and industrial targets. He designed huge, concentrated bombs and ground-penetrating 'earthquake' bombs, but he is most famous for the bouncing bombs that were capable of skipping across water surfaces like pebbles, sinking next to their targets (either battleships or dams) and acting as focused depth charges.

Delivering these bombs accurately was not easy, and the RAF's 617 Squadron (led by Guy Gibson and specially formed for an operation on the dams of the Ruhr Valley, known as Operation Chastise) had to develop their technique in many training flights. The dams in the Upper Derwent Valley were similar to the German targets, so it was here that the Dam Busters practised the difficult low-level night-time flights that would be necessary to deliver the bombs. The squadron's specially adapted Avro Lancaster bombers were a frequent sight over Derwent Reservoir in the six weeks leading up to the successful Ruhr raids on 16/17 May 1943, and the Battle of Britain Memorial Flight honours the Derwent Valley's contribution to this crucial mission with occasional Lancaster flypasts and tours of the area.

Above: Howden Dam during construction

Right: Derwent Hall before it was half-demolished and submerged beneath the waters of the Derwent Dam in 1945

Below: Bamford Edge

Walk 5: Bamford and Ladybower Reservoir

Essential Information

Distance and Approximate Walking Time: 6 miles, 3–3½ hours

Parking: Heatherdene Car Park, Ladybower Reservoir (fees applicable)

Start: Heatherdene Car Park, Ladybower Reservoir

About the Walk

This walk starts from the Heatherdene car park. We cross the Ashopton Road to the Ladybower Reservoir. The lowest of the three Derwent Reservoirs, Ladybower was constructed between 1935 and 1943 and opened by King George VI and Queen Elizabeth the Queen Mother in September 1945. We take the path over the dam wall and descend the lane to the Thornhill Cycle Trail, which follows the former trackbed of the standard-gauge railway that brought raw materials from the Hope Valley Line during the construction of the reservoirs.

One of the 'plug holes', Ladybower Reservoir

We leave the trail to take a footpath over fields towards Bamford Mill on the River Derwent. Built on the site of an earlier corn mill, the water-powered cotton mill operated from 1782. A horizontal steam engine called *Edna*, manufactured by Musgrove and Sons of Bolton, was installed at the mill in 1907, and remains in situ (though not open to the public). In the 1990s the buildings were converted into private residential apartments.

Stroll up The Hollow and cross the busy Main Road to reach the little village green, home to a memorial stone commemorating Queen Victoria's Diamond Jubilee in 1897. Heading up The Clough we leave the village behind as we ascend the old road to Bamford Moor and onto Bamford Edge, affording excellent views over the Derwent Reservoirs. Finally we descend the path below the edge and return to the car park and the end of this walk.

WALK 5: BAMFORD AND LADYBOWER RESERVOIR

Directions

1. From the Heatherdene car park, take the hard footpath just beyond the public conveniences to the Ladybower Reservoir. Follow the path for about a quarter of a mile and then descend to the road opposite the dam head wall.

2. Cross the road via the pedestrian refuge and take the path over the dam head to the opposite side. On reaching the far side of the reservoir, turn left down the lane. Before this, however, you may take a short detour by turning right to a small viewing area, giving a better view of one of the overflows below the dam wall known locally as 'plug holes'. Retrace your steps from the viewing area and walk down the lane.

3. Turn right after about 275 yards onto the waymarked Thornhill Trail.

4. Follow the trail for approximately three quarters of a mile to Carr Lane. Cross the lane to continue along the trail, passing a small car park on your right.

5. After about 400 yards the trail crosses over a farm track or lane. Take the next footpath on the left, signed to Bamford. The path descends to a track; turn right here and follow the path across the fields to reach Bamford Mill.

47

6. Walk across the footbridge and stepping stones towards the mill. Follow the path ahead between the buildings of the mill complex, and turn right and then left up The Hollow to reach the Main Road in Bamford.

7. Cross the road to the triangular green, home to the Jubilee Stone, and head up Fidlers Well away from the busy main road. Pass the Primary School and continue up The Clough.

8. Where the lane ahead is gated and marked 'Private No Entry', we follow the footpath to the right up the old road, marked on the map as Leeside Road. The path climbs steeply up the Bamford Clough to eventually join the New Road below Bamford Moor. (**Note**: an alternative route is provided on the map on the previous page, in the event that the main path is closed.)

9. Turn right and walk up the road for a short distance to the access point onto the moor on the left. Once over the stile take the path ahead that climbs straight up the moor; ignore a track on the right and any other paths off the main route. Continue on the broad path which bears left and eventually levels off as you proceed.

10. Turn left just before a stone grouse butt and walk the short distance over to the rocky cliff face of Bamford Edge. Continue in the same direction along the edge with its spectacular views over the Derwent Reservoirs. Stay left on the path close to the edge.

11. After about a mile and beyond where the path crosses over a low boundary wall, take the path almost immediately on the left which at first descends away from the edge and then bears left beneath the edge. Continue to descend on the path with an enclosed wood to your right.

12. Turn right taking a stile over a wall and fence into the wooded plantation. Continue down the path which after a while follows a clearing in the plantation before emerging above the roadside opposite the Ladybower Reservoir dam wall.

13. Turn right on the path we followed earlier to return to the car park.

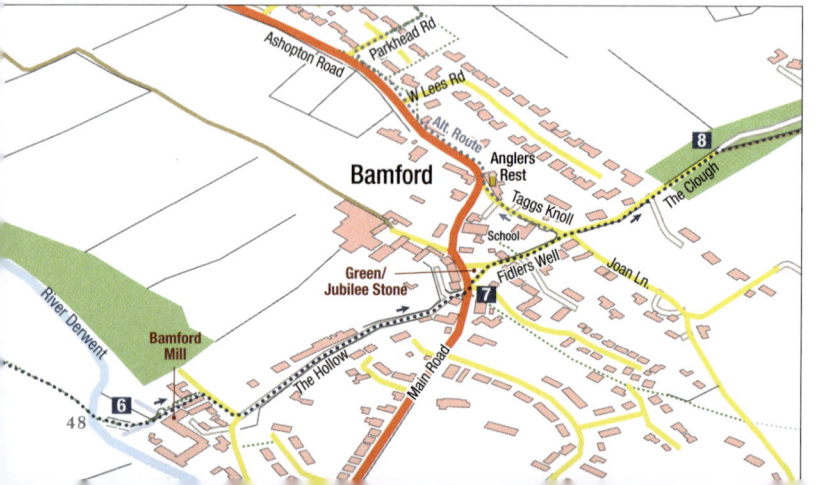

Hathersage, c. early 19th century

Hathersage

Hathersage is a village with a very long history. There are Neolithic, Bronze Age and Iron Age remains on the hills and edges surrounding the village, and it is thought there were homesteads in the valley during the Roman occupation. Crudely carved Celtic heads have been found locally; some have been built into the walls of houses, fields and churches (notably those in Bradwell and Hope), and there are two such in Hathersage. Saxon influence may be found in the shaft of a wayside cross in Hathersage churchyard, and Saxon coffin lids have also been found in the area.

The village was recorded as *Hereseige* in the Domesday Book of 1086, and by this time there were ten families in the area under the lordship of the Norman knight Ralph Fitzhubert. Two Saxon thanes, Leofnoth and Leofric, were the landowners to whom the smallholder families owed their taxes, but there was no mill, church or priest.

Hathersage's first church was built by 1135 by Richard Basset, to support the Augustinian priory of Launde Abbey in Leicestershire. The church was a simple building, enlarged and improved during the 13th and 14th centuries and completed by the addition of a spire around 1500. The current church of St Michael and All Angels was renovated in the 19th century and contains a stained-glass window salvaged from St James' Chapel in the village of Derwent, before it was lost beneath Ladybower Reservoir.

There is a strong tradition that Robin Hood lived for a time in the Hathersage area; many local landmarks bear his name, such as Robin Hood's Cross on Abney Moor and Robin Hood's Cave on Stanage Edge. The legends also suggest that his companion Little John was a local man, and he is reputed to be buried in Hathersage churchyard, in a grave near the church door. When the grave was opened in the 18th century it was found to contain a large thigh bone belonging to a man around 8 feet (2.5 metres) tall.

The Eyres were a well-known local family who lived at Padley Hall near Hathersage. They were successful businessmen with interests in local lead mines and quarries, and they were also benefactors to the village, endowing the church and contributing significantly to its expansion and improvement. By the 15th century they were employed as the agents or stewards of powerful families such as the Plumptons of Yorkshire, who had estates in Derbyshire, and the Earls of Shrewsbury. They had a reputation for high-handed actions, however, and the estates around Padley Hall were often 'improved', for example by illegal weirs, appropriating forest land and ignoring the manorial rights of others.

Hathersage Hall on School Lane mostly dates from the 17th century, converted from an older farmhouse by Robert Ashton of Castleton, a wealthy merchant with significant local lead-mining interests. The Hall passed through several generations of Ashton descendants before passing to the Spencer family in 1725, and then the Shuttleworths in 1775. Ashton Shuttleworth, known as Squire Ashton, took up residence in 1795–6; he took an active interest in the church and the (somewhat reluctant) local militia, and contributed to the improvement of local roads under the Turnpike Acts. He had interests in many local industries, and during his 36 years as Squire he presided over the village's transformation from 'a poor empty village with a button works' in the 1790s to an outward-looking settlement with transport links, a new school and an industrial future. He died in 1830; his heir, John Shuttleworth, built a fine house at Nether Hall in the early 1840s, but the family continued to live in Hathersage Hall until the mid-20th century. The building is now home to a business centre.

Hathersage was known for growing flax and hemp for processing and spinning, with rope and twine manufactured locally into the 19th century. Spinning cotton was once a household occupation, with almost every home owning a spinning wheel, but it began to be mechanised in the 18th century; by the beginning of the 19th century there were two cotton workshops in Hathersage, and a mill owned by Ashton Shuttleworth.

Stanage Edge

The village was also celebrated for its manufacture of fine needles. A wire-drawing factory was recorded as early as 1566; steel wire was needed locally to make ore baskets for mining, as well as carding combs for wool and flax/hemp. By the early 19th century wire from Hathersage was an important part of the needle industry in Redditch, and the Cook brothers came from that town in 1811 to set up in Hathersage as manufacturers of fish hooks, pins, wire, needles and other steel items. There were other wire drawers in the village, notably the staunchly Methodist Cocker family; Samuel Fox, a native of Bradwell who went on to invent the 'Paragon' steel umbrella frame, was apprenticed to Samuel Cocker from 1831 to 1834. However, ultimately the small workshops in Hathersage could not compete with the much larger outfits in Redditch, and by 1894 the Hathersage wire and needle factories had all closed.

The Eyres and other families had interests in quarrying from the Middle Ages, with local quarries producing grindstones for the metalworking trade as well as millstones. The industry continued up to the end of the 19th century, when competition from finer-quality stones brought from elsewhere and abroad, combined with the expense of moving the heavy stones, meant that the industry was no longer viable.

As elsewhere in Derbyshire there was significant lead-mining activity locally, with the remains of bole and later cupola furnaces still visible in fields. Mining declined and eventually ceased during the 19th century because of competition from abroad and the increasing technological costs of working and draining ever deeper mines; by the start of the 20th century the industry had died.

The trans-Pennine railway line linking Sheffield and Manchester (now known as the Hope Valley Line) opened in 1894, providing access into and out of the village via Hathersage Station. By this time the village was self-sufficient and busy, with tradesmen, industries, agriculture, a doctor, a bank, inns and beer houses. More recently Hathersage has become home to a cutlery factory founded by David Mellor, the influential British industrial designer, and housed in the famous Round Building on the footprint of the old gas works. The purpose-built circular factory has won a number of design awards, and the site also houses the David Mellor Design Museum, a café and a shop – well worth a visit.

North Lees Hall

Hathersage Vicarage

Charlotte Brontë and Jane Eyre

Charlotte Brontë's novel *Jane Eyre*, originally published in 1847 under the pen name Currer Bell, tells the story of the eponymous heroine and her journey from boarding school to a position as governess at Thornfield Hall, working for the enigmatic Mr Rochester. Jane falls in love with him and they almost marry, but Jane has to leave Thornfield when it comes to light that Rochester already has a wife, who is mad and whom he keeps locked in an upstairs room at the hall.

Jane's story takes many more twists and turns before she is eventually reunited with Rochester. The novel was a landmark in the history of prose fiction, being the first to focus on the moral and spiritual journey of a single character via a first-person narrative. It also contains a good deal of critical social commentary; it received a mixed response when it was published, but is now regarded as a classic.

The book has a connection with Hathersage; it is thought that Thornfield Hall was inspired by Charlotte Brontë's visits to North Lees Hall with her friend Ellen Nussey, who lived at Hathersage Vicarage. North Lees Hall has Tudor origins, built at the end of the 16th century for William Jessop and later home to the Fenton family, who had links with the Fitzherberts. It was home to the Eyre family from 1750 to 1882; Charlotte Brontë borrowed not only their surname and their family home for her novel, but also the legend of a madwoman confined in an upper room of the hall who later dies by fire.

Walk 6: Hathersage and Stanage Edge

Essential Information

Distance and Approximate Walking Time: 6½ miles, 3½–4 hours.

Parking: Oddfellows Road Car Park, Hathersage, S32 1DU (fees applicable)

Start: Oddfellows Car Park

About the Walk

This walk begins and ends in the busy village of Hathersage and takes in a variety of historic sites associated with Charlotte Brontë and the mythical figure of Robin Hood. We make our way from the village, with its numerous shops, cafés and restaurants, to the ancient church of St Michael and All Angels located in an elevated position above the modern village. The church dates from the 14th century, built on the site of a smaller church from the 12th century and an even earlier Norman church.

Inside the church are tombs and commemorative brasses to the Eyre family. In the churchyard is the reputed grave of Little John, a companion of Robin Hood, the legendary outlaw of English folklore. According to Thomas Bateman in his book *Bateman's Vestiges of the Antiquities of Derbyshire* (1848), the grave was opened in the 18th century and a thigh bone measuring 38 inches (96.5 cm) was discovered and taken to Cannon Hall in South Yorkshire, where it remained until the 1950s when it was removed into a private collection.

Adjacent to the church is Camp Green, the site of the earliest known settlement in Hathersage; this ringwork monument was probably built by Ralph Fitzhubert (1045–1086) or his successor in the early Norman period, and it is thought that the attached bailey occupied the site of the present church. From Camp Green we climb the valley side via Carr Head over Cattis-side Moor and onto Stanage Edge; this magnificent gritstone escarpment offers splendid views over the Hope Valley. We pass Robin Hood's Cave, hidden in the rocks just below the path.

In 1845 Charlotte Brontë stayed at the vicarage in Hathersage, visiting her school friend Ellen Nussey. Brontë was inspired by her visit to Hathersage, and the village became the fictional Morton in her famous novel *Jane Eyre* (1847). On the return leg of our walk we pass North Lees Hall, the former home of the Eyre family, which became Mr Rochester's Thornfield Hall.

Directions

1. Take the footpath from the car park, and pass the Methodist Church to reach the Main Road. Cross the road via the pedestrian crossing, turn right and walk up the pedestrian channel on the left, passing The Bank.

2. At the junction with Hall Cottage in front of you, turn left along Baulk Lane.

3. Take the next footpath on the right opposite the cricket ground, leading to the church.

4. Follow the path to St Michael and All Angels' church. Just beyond the doorway to the church on the right is the reputed grave of Little John. Continue along the path and exit the churchyard via the lychgate.

Little John's grave and church, Hathersage

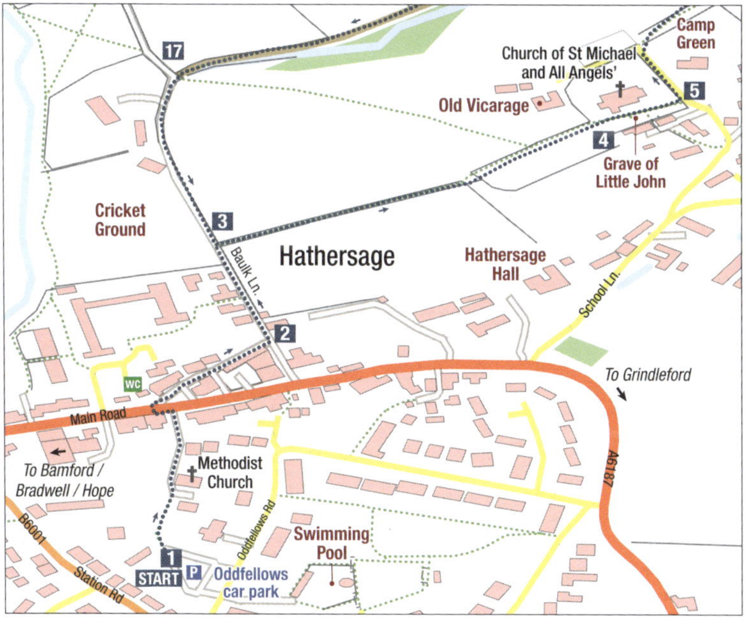

5. Turn left up the lane and take the footpath ahead. Follow the footpath to the right that skirts around the perimeter of Camp Green (ignore the path that descends on the left). Camp Green is an scheduled ancient monument and a rare example of a Norman ringwork or fortification. The path leads to a narrow lane, where we turn left and walk uphill.

6. Continue up the lane without deviation for about a third of a mile to Carr Head Farm, passing a vineyard on your left prior to the farm.

7. Just beyond the main building the path turns off the drive to the right and climbs away from the farm. Go through a farm gate and continue straight up the hill to Leveret Lane below Cattis-side Moor.

8. Turn left and walk along the lane. Pass Leveret Croft and take the next footpath on the right. Go straight up the path, which skirts to the right of Carrhead Rocks and then over the moor to the road.

9. At the road, turn left and walk to Hook's Carr car park at the side of the lane on the left. Walk a short way down the car park and take the footpath on the right leading up onto Stanage Edge.

10. Turn left along the edge. After about 300 yards, Robin Hood's Cave is hidden in the rocks below the path. Continue for approximately half a mile to a stile over a fence at the end of a stone wall. Walk a short distance further to leave the edge via the path off to the left, adjacent to a distinctive rocky outcrop.

11. The path quickly doubles back and descends into woods. Beyond the woods, where the path forks bear left to reach the road.

12. Take the footpath on the opposite side of the road to Hathersage. There are public conveniences on the right. The path bears to the left and descends to join a track. Turn right down the track, and at the bottom of the woods go through a gate then continue on the path down the field to North Lees Hall.

13. Go through the gate and turn left down the track; North Lees Hall is on the other side of the wall. Follow the drive all the way down to Birley Road.

14. Cross the road and take the stile almost opposite over the stone wall. Turn

Cattis-side-Moor

Hathersage

right on the track, and then turn left off the track to follow the waymarked path that skirts around Cow Close Farm.

15. When the path opens up with a view of the church in the distance, follow a waymarker towards the fence (field boundary) and walk downhill, keeping the fence on your right to join with another path at the bottom of the field.

16. Turn right and follow the track to Baulk Lane.

17. Turn left along Baulk Lane to the cricket ground, and from here retrace your steps back to the car park on Oddfellows Road.

Grindleford, Padley and Longshaw

The village of Grindleford takes its name from the site of a medieval ford, created by sinking millstones (grindles) in the River Derwent. It is 7 miles from the centre of Sheffield and less than 3 miles from Totley at the other end of the Totley Tunnel, 3.5 miles long and at the time of its completion in 1893 the second-longest rail tunnel in the UK. Grindleford Station, about a mile from the village, opened in 1894 at the western portal of the tunnel to facilitate the transport of stone from local quarries. However, the coming of the railway also opened up Grindleford, Padley and the Hope Valley to day trippers and commuters from Sheffield, changing a handful of isolated agricultural settlements into a popular and thriving tourist destination.

Padley Hall was built around 1400, on the banks of the River Derwent near Grindleford Bridge. It was owned by the Padley family, but passed by marriage to the locally notorious Eyre family, and then to the staunchly Catholic Fitzherberts, who came in for religious persecution during the reign of Queen Elizabeth I. Sir Thomas Fitzherbert was imprisoned for his faith in 1559, and Padley Hall and North Lees Hall in Hathersage were both raided in 1588; two priests, Robert Ludlam and Nicholas Garlick, were discovered in hiding and arrested along with Sir Thomas's brother John Fitzherbert and his family, as well as their servants and estate workers. They were all taken to Derby and thrown into the county gaol.

Padley Chapel

Longshaw Lodge, when it was a Holiday Fellowship Guest House

The two priests were tried at Derby Assizes, found guilty of high treason and executed by hanging, drawing and quartering near St Mary's Bridge in Derby. Sir Thomas and John Fitzherbert both died in prison in London in the early 1590s, and Padley Hall passed through a number of hands up to 1657, when it was sold to pay debts and apparently never lived in again. It was eventually pulled down, although the gatehouse remained standing.

In 1898 a public pilgrimage was arranged to honour Robert Ludlam and Nicholas Garlick, the Padley Martyrs, and in 1933 the gatehouse was converted into a Catholic chapel in their honour, with the rescued altar stone from the original chapel installed and newly consecrated. The pilgrimage has taken place every year since 1898, and Ludlam and Garlick were beatified by Pope John Paul II in 1987.

The Longshaw Estate is a 747-acre area of woodland, moorland and farmland to the north-east of Grindleford and Padley, stretching from Burbage and White Edge down to the River Derwent in the valley below. The area is criss-crossed by packhorse routes and trackways, and was once a busy centre of industry; traces of activities such as quarrying, leadworking and charcoal burning can all be spotted in the landscape. Now managed by the National Trust, the estate is a tranquil haven for wildlife and plants. Longshaw Lodge, on the estate and now comprising private residential accommodation, was built around 1827 as a 'shooting box' for John Henry Manners, the 5th Duke of Rutland, who was the landowner at that time. White Edge Lodge, once a gamekeeper's cottage, is now holiday accommodation managed by the National Trust.

Padley Gorge

Walk 7: Grindleford Station, Padley Gorge and Longshaw Estate

Essential Information

Distance and Approximate Walking Time: 5 miles, 2½–3½ hours

Parking: Nr. Grindleford Station, Station Approach, Grindleford (fees applicable)

Start: Grindleford Station Café

About the Walk

Starting at the Grindleford Station Café we make our way over the railway bridge towards Padley Mill; this attractive 18th century water-powered corn mill is now a private residence. Further along the lane we pass Padley Chapel, the former gatehouse to the Elizabethan Padley Hall. The foundations of the old hall can be seen at the rear of the chapel.

We follow the path through Bolehill Wood; this is now a peaceful natural environment, but the scene was very different in the early 20th century when production at Bolehill Quarry prompted a mini-boom in the population of the local area. One and a quarter million tons of gritstone went from here to build the nearby Howden and Derwent Dams. Standard-gauge locomotives were used to transport stone from the quarry face to the top of a steep incline, down which the heavy stone-laden wagons descended to the Midland Railway (now known as the Hope Valley Line) via a balanced incline. The weight of the laden wagons was used to haul empties back up to the quarry. The site closed in 1914 and is now managed by the National Trust.

The footpath climbs Padley Gorge through ancient woodland onto moorland at Lawrence Field. There are remains of a medieval enclosure and two associate long houses on Lawrence Field, and there is also a stone circle of undetermined age consisting of four standing stones.

Our next destination is Longshaw Lodge, built for the 5th Duke of Rutland in 1827 and used as a shooting lodge. The Jacobean-style lodge has a stable block and a coach house, with a free-standing chapel added in 1890. The interior is now converted into private residential accommodation. We continue on formal footpaths and over open pasture on the Longshaw Estate before descending woodland and crossing the B6521 to a footpath that returns us to the Grindleford Station Café.

Longshaw Estate

Padley Mill

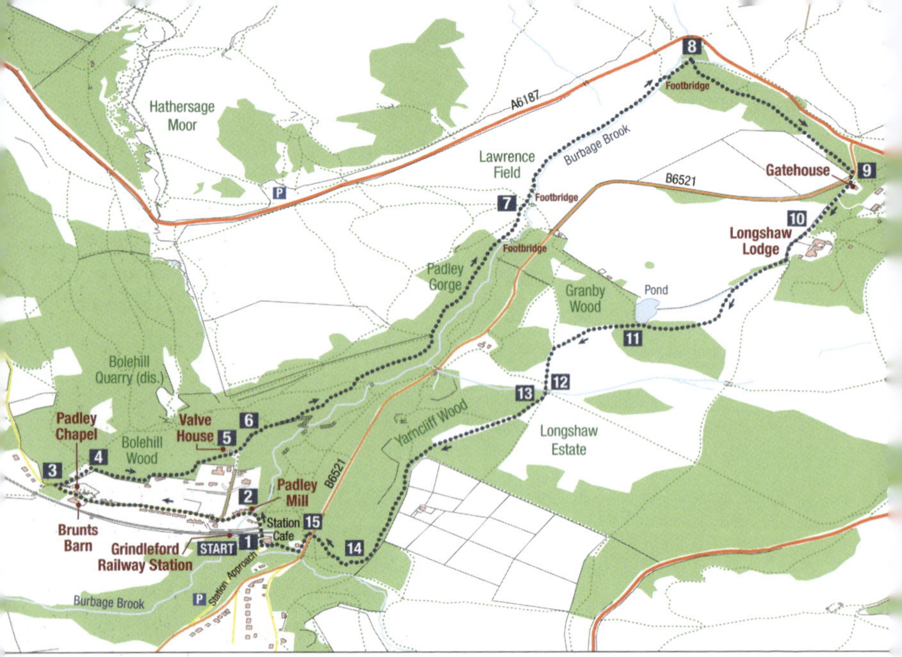

Directions

1. Starting from the station café, walk towards the railway over the bridge. Look over the parapet on your right to see the western portal of Totley Tunnel. Continue ahead to a private road, and follow the footpath along it. After a narrow road bridge where the Burbage Brook runs through the gorge we pass Padley Mill.

2. Continue on the lane (Windses Estate). Ignore a turning on the right for the Longshaw Estate, instead continuing until you reach Brunts Barn and Padley Chapel. The 14th-century gatehouse to Padley Hall is now a Roman Catholic chapel; the foundation walls of the old hall survive at the rear of the chapel.

3. Stay on the lane for about 40 yards beyond the chapel to a cattle grid, and then turn right onto the footpath. Pass

Station Café, Grindleford

through a couple of gates and begin to climb the hillside away from the lane. The path then follows a stone boundary wall on your right; ignore a path to the left and continue uphill, keeping close to the wall.

4. Turn right at the top edge of the wall on the path that traverses Bolehill Wood. Follow the boundary around several dwellings.

62

5. We join another path just below a large stone building with a domed roof. This is a valve house on the aqueduct carrying water from the Derwent dams. Follow the path ahead in the same direction, passing the valve house on your left side. We join another well-defined partly cobbled path; after a short distance, just off the path there is a red-brick building with an arched entrance and roof. This was a gunpowder store for the Bolehill Quarry.

6. Continue along the path, following the course of Burbage Brook to the top of Padley Gorge (half a mile). Do not deviate from the main path, ignoring the turning for Surprise View and Bole Hill Quarry. Near the top of the gorge, after passing through a gate we emerge out of the woodland onto open moorland at Lawrence Field.

7. Do not cross the brook via the lower footbridges; instead, continue following the course of Burbage Brook (on your right) for about a third of a mile to another footbridge prior to the road (A6187). Cross the footbridge and ascend the path through the woods.

8. Turn sharp right to stay on the partly cobbled path where a stream tumbles down through the woods and passes beneath the footpath. Stay on this path for just over a third of a mile to its end, a stile that leads directly onto the road (B6521).

9. Cross the stile and turn right down the road. Not far on the other side of the road is a bus stop and the entrance gates to Longshaw Lodge (NT). Cross the road here, pass the gatehouse and walk up the drive towards the lodge.

10. Prior to the lodge, leave the drive and turn right onto the footpath. Pass the front elevation of Longshaw Lodge. Go through a wooden gate and turn immediately right on the hard footpath and follow it towards a large pond.

11. At the edge of the pond, take the first footpath on the left. There is a wooden fingerpost signed to Yarncliff, and a little further on is a wooden gate leading to open pasture. Follow the path ahead, which descends and eventually joins a track. Turn left along the track.

12. At a junction of paths where a stream runs down the hillside and goes beneath the track, we continue straight ahead.

13. After no more than 40 yards, turn onto a path that bears right and follow it for about 360 yards to reach a gate at the edge of a wood. Follow the path along the top edge of Yarncliff Wood.

14. Descend through the woods along an obvious path on the right. As you walk down there are stone steps to help with your descent. (**Note**: if you reach a stone wall and gate before descending, you have missed the turn.) Follow the path down all the way to the road (B6521).

15. Cross the road, turn left and walk a few yards down the pavement, and then take the next footpath on the right to bring you back to Grindleford Station Café and the end of this walk.

Bibliography

Adam, W. (1838) *The Gem of the Peak*. London: Longman & Co.

Archaeological Research Services website, www.archaeologicalresearchservices.com

Vicus adjacent to Navio Roman fort (Projects/Hope Shale Quarry)

Bateman, T. (1845) *Vestiges of the Antiquities of Derbyshire*. London:

Bateman, T. (1861) *Ten Years Digging in Celtic and Saxon Grave Hills in the Counties of Derby, Stafford and York from 1848 to 1858*. London: Smith.

Buxton, B.A. (2005) *Hathersage in the Peak: A history*. Chichester: Phillimore.

Clarke, L. (2009) *Castleton: A history, a tour, people, buildings and industries*. Castleton: Owl Publishing.

Derbyshire Historic Environment website, her.derbyshire.gov.uk
- Chapel to Longshow Lodge (list entry MDR12504)
- Mam Tor Hill fort, Castleton (list entry MDR2223)
- Possible Romano-British settlement, Bradwell Hills (list entry MDR10080)
- Roman quern built into fireplace in Brough (list entry MDR2393)

Dodd, A.E. & Dodd, E.M. (1974) *Peakland Roads and Trackways*. Hartington: Moorland Publishing Co.

Evans, S. (1912) *Bradwell: Ancient and Modern*. Printed by subscription.

Ford, T. (2004) *Rocks and Scenery of the Peak District*. Ashbourne: Landmark Publishing Ltd.

Ford, T. (2019) *Derbyshire Blue John* (3rd edition, edited by T. Waltham and N. Worley). Nottingham: East Midlands Geological Society.

Gifford, A. (1999) *Derbyshire Watermills: Corn mills*. Midland Wind and Water Mills Group.

Harris, H. (1971) *Industrial Archaeology of the Peak District*. Ashbourne: Ashbourne Editions.

Historic England website, www.historicengland.org.uk
- Hathersage Hall (list entry 1109807)
- Hope Motte (list entry 1017661)
- Navio Roman fort and vicus (list entry 1017505)
- Slight univallate hillfort and two bowl barrows on Mam Tor (list entry 1011206)
- The Grey Ditch (list entry 1017662)

Jackson, A.A. (2000) *The Railway Dictionary: An A–Z of railway terminology*. Stroud: Sutton.

Leyland, J. (1891) *The Peak of Derbyshire: Its scenery and antiquities*. London: Seeley & Co.

Maskill, L. (2021) *The Spa Waters of Derbyshire*. Buxton: Curlew Press.

Naylor, P.J. (1983) *Ancient Wells and Springs of Derbyshire*. Cromford: Scarthin Books.

Naylor, P.J. (1983) *Celtic Derbyshire*. Derby: Hall & Sons Ltd.

Rieuwerts, J.H. (2007) *Lead Mining in Derbyshire: History, Development and Drainage, Vol 1: Castleton to the River Wye*. Ashbourne: Landmark Publishing Ltd.

Small, C. (2004) *Bamford Living Memory: A hundred years of life in a Peak District village*. Bamford: Bamford Community Arts and Crafts.

Smith, H. (2019) *The Mortimer Road: The turnpike road that failed*. Howard Smith.

Ward, R. (1827) *A Guide to the Peak of Derbyshire*. Birmingham: W. Ward (Printer).